This Isn't It

Reviving the Woman Within

Curtrice L. Williams

Jeanius Publishing LLC
PO Box 1562
Lehigh Acres, FL 33936

jeaniuspublishing.com
gentlewomenhood.com

For more information, please visit:
jeaniuspublishing.com; or
inquiry@jeaniuspublishing.com

ISBN-13: 978-0-9974265-0-2

Cover design: Omar Rodriguez
Editor: Elizabeth Morgan Garner
Illustration: TreManda Pewett
Photography: Eric Dejuan (Eric Dejuan Photography)
Stylist: Daniel Grier (Splashed by DKG)
Hair Stylist: Desiree McNabb
Makeup Artist: Latoya Eaton (FacePro Makeup Artistry)

Dedication

To my son, Aedan Kenyon Grier, you have been a constant reminder of God's love for me and have introduced me to true and unconditional love. You are the beautiful reason behind my determination to never give up.

To my parents, you nurtured me and raised me with great care. I will forever be grateful for your love, sacrifices, and the beautiful example of not only what true love looks like but also what it does. Thank you so much for contributing to the woman I am today.

To my brother, you have always been there for me and everything you do reflects your heart of gold. Thank you for everything you've done for your nephew and for me.

In loving memory of my late brother Bert, I know if you were here you would be proud of me. I'm so grateful to have had you in my life as long as I did. You loved so hard just like I do and even through the tragedy that took your life I learned life lessons that I will always hold dear to my heart. I love you and will forever miss you.

To Daniel Grier, thank you for believing in me. I am grateful for all of our years of friendship and the wisdom, clarity, grace, and mercy with which God has blessed us. No matter what shifts we have experienced in our relationship, we have held on tightly to a bond that I cherish. That bond has been responsible for so much of our growth as individuals and as parents. For that bond I will forever be thankful.

To Amelia Grier, I am so grateful for the relationship we have. You have showed me unconditional love and been there to help and pray for me through some of the roughest times I've experienced in life. For that and the bond we share I will be forever grateful and thankful.

To LeAnn Marsh, thank you for being the sister that I never had. You have prayed for me and been there for me so much over the years. We have grown up together and I cherish our friendship. I will be forever grateful for your special place in my life.

To Pierre Alex Jeanty, thank you for just being you. You are the type of person who is driven, and strives, to be the change you want to see in the world. You have taught me so much. I will forever be grateful to you for the help and advice you have humbly provided to me and the positive people to whom you have introduced me.

To Napolian Barnes, Priscilla Williams, and Adara Butler, each of you has touched my life in your own special way and I can't thank you enough for the blessing that you have been, and continue to be, to me.

Contents

Introduction

I would love to be able to tell you only good things and let this book be all about how everything will be easy. But because I have experienced differently and I understand that the process involves the bad and the ugly as well, instead of sugar coating things I just want to tell you that there's hope. Right now things may feel impossible, they may feel incredibly in shambles, and you may just feel like curling into a ball and crying the rest of your life away.

But no matter how attractive it might seem, crying your life away is not the answer. First let me say, it is perfectly okay to have your moment. You are human and you have feelings, and let's be real, some things can really just break your heart. But at this very moment, whether you realize it or not, the ball is still in your court. You have a choice to give up and it's your choice, no one's choice but yours. But at the very same time, you have the choice to accept whatever has happened and move forward from it. So often I hear people say "it's easier said than done" and yes, that's true. But moving forward is possible and possibility is all you need.

Nobody ever said that it would be easy and, quite honestly, you may find yourself having hard times more than you'd like. One thing is for sure though, if you can learn to have your moment, pray, and say "okay this is what it is, this is where I am, this is how it has to be right now" and follow it by "but I will not give up!"

you're well on your way to stepping into some of the best days of your life.

Unfortunately, those days may not be tomorrow or the next day, but you *will* feel an instant change in how you feel when you change your perspective. It's like being forced to live in a box and wanting so badly to be free but understanding and accepting that at this instant you're not so you begin to look at it all through a different lens. You begin to decorate; you begin to make the very best of the space you inhabit since you live there now. You decide to be happy because your life is precious and you begin to tell yourself that you can, and will, make it through. All the while you are gaining precious strength and learning vital lessons that prepare you for the day when you no longer live in that box.

*Sometimes we find **ourselves** doing things we never imagined we would be doing, maybe even things we don't want to do. There are things that are hard. There are things that hurt. There are things that are very unfortunate and things that we may look back on and realize we brought upon ourselves. But ultimately we have a choice to either give up or to keep pushing forward.*

Chapter 1

The Single Mother

Maybe you are a single mother raising your kid(s) alone, or at least for the most part, and doing the very best you can. Waking up and having a wonderful husband and father or father figure for your children would be nice, right? After going through what you have it's like, "yes, if only things were really that simple." Instead, you wake up to another day full of responsibilities, another day of maybe feeling like you're not enough, another day of loving your child so much and so badly wishing you had more to offer them.

Now that we have discussed some of the negative feelings, allow me to shed a little light. You're a mother, that in itself is something thousands of women pray every day to be and yet God blessed you to be a mother. So no matter how hard it may be, please know and understand that you are so blessed to have a child who calls you "mommy" and for whom you are enough. While the situation may not be ideal, you are not alone. It's on those rough days that you need to just start counting every single blessing you can think of, starting with the fact that you and your child had air in your lungs when you woke up this morning.

Being a mother has been one of the biggest blessings of my life. My son has been the reason behind so much of my growth and there are times that I look at him and just thank God for allowing me to be a mother to such a phenomenal little boy. There are also times that I look at him and ask God to help me. As a woman, I am aware of the motherly characteristics that God placed within me, and there are times where I feel like those things really need strengthening. It's not easy raising a child in a single parent household. Sometimes it can be a constant battle in your mind, and with your emotions. It's easy to feel defeated at times.

It's easy to focus on what you feel like you can't do and provide versus what you can do and are already providing. It's easy to forget who you truly are in the midst of this mental battle. You are so much to those eyes that look up to you. While you're beating yourself up, your child is doing the complete opposite. They are giving you every reason to find peace and exude joy.

Children are so innocent and you have to remember that they see us through the eyes of innocence. As a single mother, sometimes you might forget that they don't know the whole story, they don't understand certain things yet. So while you're worrying about things you can't change, they're just grateful to have you. But if you spend too much time worrying and stressing, those negative vibes will be passed on to them and you will begin to notice it in their behavior. Those nine months you spent nurturing them inside of you created a lifelong bond. They ate what you ate, they went wherever you went, and they even felt what you felt. After birth the umbilical cord was cut and that physically separated you but don't think that they won't always have very heightened senses when it comes to you and that's something that lasts as long as you live. It's important to take care of yourself, not just physically, but mentally, emotionally, and spiritually as well. By doing those things you will have peace and be able to be the best mother you can be.

Sometimes people place the title "single mother" in a box. Every single mom isn't doing it all on her own. Some of us co-parent, and that can come with its own challenges at times, but it is vital to always keep your child's best interest at heart. No matter what the circumstances are now, you and your child's father created another life and you both are responsible for raising the life you created. An unhealed heart, selfishness, pride, bitterness, and a lack of good communication unfortunately are some of the main reasons why so many children grow up hating one parent or living without them in their life at all. You have to commit to not allowing any of those things to step in the way of doing what's right. It may not always be easy but that in no way means it's impossible.

You need to consistently do your part, and understand that it requires working on the woman you are within. You shouldn't act on just your emotions. You shouldn't get upset with him and create a wedge between him and your child. That will always hurt your child the most. Things don't always go the way we desire, and you have to look at things and accept your part in the result versus only pointing fingers in the other direction. That's the only way you will grow from what you experience, and growing *from* something is the only way to grow *into* something and someone greater. This is your life. You need to take control and that begins with accepting who you are where you are.

Your child may not understand right now, but what you're doing for them, in all aspects, is molding them into the type of adult they will be. So each time you're handling a difficult situation, remember that the way you respond to difficulties is teaching them how to respond to them. That alone should be enough to cause you to work on making whatever necessary changes within yourself to ensure that you're setting the best example. There is no real-time instruction manual with every single thing you will face while being a mother and you will not know exactly how to do it, but it's something that you can surely work hard at each day.

Motherhood is an endless journey of learning. You must embrace all of its many facets and learn to not be so hard on yourself. If you are doing the best you can, don't stop, and most importantly, don't lose your faith. By now you know every day won't be easy but every day you are gaining more strength and knowledge. It's important to cherish all of this time you have and not waste it away wishing things were different. Instead make right now as wonderful as you can and continue to believe in God for His greatest for you and your family.

Part of being a mother is being strong, being resilient, and always working towards being better. There isn't a handbook in the world that will prepare you for the ups and the downs, the smiles and the frowns. So to all of you mothers out there, please continue to own your crown. You are a Queen responsible for raising royalty.

A mother's love is so beautiful. In it lies such great strength and a bond like no other, the very true meaning of unconditional. It doesn't come with a step-by-step guide but thank God for being there every step of the way. Mothers are beautiful and resilient gems who reflect God's love to this world.

You don't have to have it all together to be happy or joyful. Embrace right where you are WHILE you get it together.

She felt like she failed; failed herself, failed the little set of eyes that look up to her. She felt like no matter what she did it was never enough. Wondering why she was still where she was after all of her hard work, she wept, but it wasn't the end. She would keep pushing.

Chapter 2

The Woman Experiencing A Setback

Maybe you're experiencing a major life setback. This can truly be a trying time. It seems like your mind is constantly being filled with so many negative thoughts and the idea of just throwing in the towel crosses your mind more than ever. But don't. No matter what you may be going through, whether it is losing a job, a serious financial hardship, a failed business, loss of transportation, a serious illness, or any other similar crisis; it's still not the end. Now is the time to become committed to believing in who you are. Now is the time to be serious about that choice we discussed; it's yours!

We tend to spend the majority of our time during a setback trying to figure it all out on our own but this is a sure way to become majorly depressed and to dig a deeper hole than we already feel stuck in. Take this time to be grateful for the small things and embrace everything that's going right even if what's going right seems small in comparison. It's just a matter of balancing your attention so that you can begin to think clearer and make choices that will benefit you rather than bring you down. Once you are thinking clearer you'll have more energy to continue your job search, search for services that can help you until you're more financially stable, get back to the drawing board with your business, allow people to help you until you're able to have your own transportation again, and strengthen your faith in God during it all. When we are only focusing on the negative we often do things that can block our blessings, which in turn keeps us where we are longer than may be necessary.

Give yourself some time to process whatever setback you're experiencing, have your moment, but never lose your faith. All of the things we experience open up a door to learning vital lessons that will be blessings to us in the future. At the time it may be the very last thing you want to hear but it's true and should be considered. You are worthy of wonderful things and although the journey has gotten tough it doesn't mean it always will be that way. As long as you are living and breathing there is hope and that should be a fact that you never forget.

*Imagine if it hurt this time like it did
the last,
If you didn't grow from the things you
learned in your past.*

*What if your journey had no obstacles
and the road was smooth?*

*Do you realize that all of that would
change you?*

*You wouldn't have grown to be the
strong woman you are.
You wouldn't have learned to be
confident, even with scars.
So be grateful for the tough experience
called growth
Because it taught you to understand
your worth.*

When it all comes crashing down faith is all I have. I can see that everything is wrong but I know it will be made right. I don't know when or even how, but I'm sure of it. I wipe away tears and I face fears, accepting that I have faced some of my greatest fears already. Still, it's not the end. I live through it. Every day I wake up I know it's not over, I will win, I have a purpose. God isn't done with me yet.

Behind all of those negative thoughts is a positive woman and behind that doubt is confidence. Inside your heart is desire. You have hopes, dreams, and aspirations. You are phenomenal and the moment you believe in yourself is the moment you begin to break free from everything that will hold you back.

I believe we all have it in us but not everyone makes the decision to fight for what they want and actually stick with it. Sticking with it requires a great deal of discipline and faith, even if it's just the size of a mustard seed.

Bit by bit she worked to get it together, and she did. Now things are better. Still sometimes she would slip up and fall but she never let that keep her down at all. She knew she had a purpose and whatever it took to live it out was worth it.

Chapter 3

The Woman Who Is Stuck

Have you ever found yourself in a situation that literally feels impossible to get out of? Maybe you made poor choices and now look around and find yourself tied to people and situations that are only bringing you down. Maybe your life has taken a turn and you must turn with it but without the people and things you desire. Maybe you're confused about where you are in life because you don't know what to do although you have goals and you have dreams that you've yet to live. Things happen. It's important to know that although you're overwhelmed, the fact that you can see that you're somewhere you don't belong means you're in better shape than you may presently feel.

At this point it literally becomes so much about knowing your worth. One of the hardest things to understand at a time like this is that although you may have made poor choices and done things that you're not proud of, you are still valuable. And you begin accepting and acting out this value the moment you say "no" to settling where you have for too long. Everything that feels good isn't good for you. Everything that looks good isn't good for you. And everything you may have put into the wrong people or things still isn't worth it.

When you opt to stay you should really understand what you're doing. We have this one life and it's precious. When we stay in a place that is only tearing us down or only feeding the fleshly areas of our life we literally begin withering away day by day. It becomes an addiction and anything it may have once been goes out of the window. You have to recognize exactly what it is right now and make a decision to continue living beneath what you truly deserve or commit to going through the process of letting go no matter how hard it may be.

Let's talk in terms of relationships. I have been there. I have been stuck in my own personal situations so please know that I am not just saying what sounds good. I didn't want to move on from the things, and very deeply in my case a *person*, I loved so deeply. You might be saying "But Curtrice you don't understand! I have never loved a man so deeply. I have never given so much of myself. I have never been so disappointed and discouraged." Well, to that I say, "I never had either." I had loved before but never had I loved so unconditionally. Never had I effortlessly felt so selfless. Never had I stared what my heart desired in the face and then watched as it all came crashing down. But it all happened and I was so stuck there.

It was a dark, cold, painful time and it's easy to feel like people don't get it in times like those. Like just because the things that you're experiencing happen every day you're supposed to just brush it off easily and move on. You feel like you can't just move on easily from the man who you'd do anything for, the man whose head you know without a shadow of doubt you'd hold up if he ever found himself unable to do so himself. If he

26

ever found himself unable to walk you would help him get around and when you could, you would be his legs. That type of love isn't formed every day, you don't just feel that way overnight. So it's easy to feel stuck; you just want everything to be okay. You're not ready to give up. You want to fight harder.

For me, now looking back on it, what sticks out most is that I wasn't supposed to just move on *easily*. It wasn't supposed to be a time where it wasn't painful. What I was missing was that it was supposed to be a time where I trusted God more than I ever had. It was supposed to be a time where I gave it all to Him and took my hands out of it. It was supposed to be a time where I concentrated on what I needed to do for *myself*, where I reevaluated *myself* and changed my perspective. It was supposed to be a time where I remembered that I was a Queen. A time where I held on to my worth, where I looked at the choices I made and learned from it all. It was supposed to be a time of growth and healing; a time where I refused to drown in the feelings of confusion, guilt, and self-consciousness. There was so much I could have done differently to be freed sooner but I was too focused on myself to see that then. I didn't trust God like I said I was or would because if I had I wouldn't have spent so much time being broken and depressed, stuck. I admit that God was trying so hard to show me that all I needed to do was trust Him, that He knew what He was allowing to happen and He knew why. But day in and day out my focus was on what I wanted instead of what I needed, which was to trust Him.

Don't be like me. Try placing your focus on the fact that it's time to trust your journey like never before. Once you pour your heart out it's time to begin healing. You will experience freedom from all of the things that once had you bound. You won't cry everyday anymore. You won't breakdown at random times throughout the day. You won't feel like your future won't be beautiful because you will know that it will, and at the end of the day that's so worth it. It's all a part of growth. When you begin exercising real faith, each day gets a little easier. Each day your eyes will begin to get their shine back. You will begin to be so much more confident. It will be life changing.

She was lost and found more than once. She would make bad choices, break and rebuild, get hurt again and again and heal. One day she decided enough was enough. She had to take a different road and it would be tough. She saw that it would mean spending a lot of time by herself and learning to just appreciate what she had left.

As you work to reach your goals, you'll be met with resistance. You'll lose people. You'll lose things, but it'll all be worth it when you're living your dreams.

When it comes to relationships, the reality is very real and serious. So many Queens are stuck, trapped, and unsure of what to do because all they know is that they love him with everything they have but he may not be there yet or the feelings may not be as deep for him. He may not want a family, to settle down, and be with one woman forever. If this is you then likely all you know is that this is all *you* want, so it hurts. It's time for the chains to be broken because you deserve a relationship where you're there because you both don't want to do life apart. Where you love each other unconditionally and look forward to growing old and laughing until you lose your breath. Never settle and don't remain stuck.

No matter what your situation is, feeling stuck will take the life right out of you. You'll begin to lose your glow and resort to trying to hide behind a smile so it won't show. But if you don't face it all now then you'll never grow.

Chapter 4

The Woman Who Misses The Past

You're human, with feelings and desires, and, truth be told, sometimes from where we see it parts of our past were some of the very best days of our lives. So to be right where you are and conscious that you truly miss the way things used to be is okay. It's not okay to stay here forever though. Things happen, people change, we change, people come, people go, great things turn into even greater things, and good things go bad. All sorts of things can happen in time.

Right now may be one of the hardest times for you though. Sometimes you can miss people and things so much that you block yourself from ever experiencing happiness again. Don't let yourself fall into that trap. Although the road ahead may be a hard and uncomfortable one, you don't want to remain right where you are. You don't want to keep crying tears and constantly feeling like there's a void. That's not living! That is just existing here on this earth and I get it, you probably feel like you can't even help it, but I'm here to tell you that you can, and you will, if you truly commit to doing so. First, ask yourself this one question, "At this very moment what can I do to completely change things?" That answer starts with you. You can change things but understand that it may not be in the way you desire at this moment.

Things only change when our thinking changes. Maybe at this moment you miss someone you once shared so much of yourself with and, for whatever reason, it came to an end. That is a moment in which our minds become filled with so many negative thoughts that our hearts literally hurt. It's not easy, and I'm definitely not here to tell you that it is, but the one thing you have to understand is tomorrow will come and go and so will the next day and if you don't allow yourself to begin healing that time won't come for you. Instead, you will remain in a state of depression constantly replaying those precious moments you so passionately hold dear within.

I've been there and I know that without true faith and a real desire to get better I would still be exactly how I once was. I didn't want to eat, I didn't sleep well. I cried every day. I faked a smile. I asked myself millions of questions. I tried so hard to fix things and I blamed myself. I questioned God, I begged God. I pretended like everything was still the same. I refused to accept things for what they were. I was a mess. I did so many things just wishing so badly that things had gone the way my heart desired but the reality was always still the very same.

One of the biggest things you can do wrong is not accept the truth. I encourage you to use the lines below to write the exact thing that has happened, who you miss and why, and after you write it say it out loud.

_____

_____

_____

_____

_____

_____

_____

_____

_____

_____

_____

_____

_____

_____.

Now that you have written down your feelings, you need to truly be able to begin accepting that it happened and be okay with not being okay at this moment. You don't have to fake it to make it because you won't truly be making it anywhere. Don't be fooled by that way of thinking. I encourage you to be okay with how you feel but to also begin pouring positive affirmations into yourself daily. Use the lines below to write down some very positive things about yourself and your life. I want you to visit this page regularly and remind yourself of these things because sometimes the more you begin trying to think positively, the more things begin to happen to make you forget what previously seemed so desperately important to you.

1._____

_____

_____

_____.

2._____

_____

_____

_____.

3._____

_____

_____

_____.

4._____

_____

_____

_____.

Let me be the first to tell you that if it wasn't for more prayers than I could ever count and consistently falling and getting back up and trying again on my journey I wouldn't be here to tell you any of this. So if you are a spiritual person I encourage you to kick your prayer life into hyper-drive. God is the one who never gets tired of listening to us and the one who can understand us even when we don't understand ourselves. He knows your most intimate desires and on those days when you feel like you can't keep going, He will be your strength. I never really got angry at God but I did cry my eyes out asking "why me?" Now I look at it like "why not me?" Bad things happen to good people all of the time and the strength that I have gained over the years from different experiences has in itself spoken volumes to me.

We have to understand that things don't always go the way we desire for them to go, but if we continue to keep pushing and allowing God to shape and mold us, we will, without a shadow of a doubt, be taken care of in all areas. So get up, get out, enjoy the family and friends you have, and if you feel like you have no one, you are in the perfect position to begin loving yourself like you never have before. Remember that we often attract what we put out so if you begin to put out good to others in time you will begin to attract some good people as well.

Remember too that you are not equal to your circumstances. Just because you have lost someone dear to you and are having a hard time coping doesn't mean that you're an unworthy person or that you aren't enough for someone to love and appreciate. That is one of the biggest mistakes we make, feeling like nothing because we lost something. Please don't do that because you are something and recognizing and accepting that you *are* something starts within you. Once you truly believe that you are a person worthy of love and respect you won't settle for people who don't show you that they know you are worthy as well. You will begin to make better choices and you will be in better shape to determine if someone's actions are consistent with their words.

More than likely this won't be the last time you miss the way things once were, but once you truly heal from where you are now, it makes the other times easier to bear. You gain clarity and you understand yourself better. Right now you are becoming stronger whether you see it or not, and trust me when I say that strength will come in handy as you experience other things in life. Don't use this time to beat yourself up and call yourself stupid because you're not. Use this time to face reality, accept your truth, and heal.

It hurt her.

She wondered how she could be so amazing but be treated as if she was not enough,

How she was worth holding on to but cut loose by the ones she loved the most.

She wondered why God allowed her heart to be so incredibly broken.

And why HIS word said one thing but she was experiencing another.

She wondered why she was forced into uncomfortable situations and why things couldn't just be easier.

She wondered, it hurt her.

She wouldn't change a thing.

It hurt; there were times she felt like giving up. It was painful, there were times she cried long and hard but now she wouldn't change a thing. What she has been through molded her into who she is today and she loves that woman. She loved that man so much that she gave it all to God. She wouldn't change a thing but left in the hands of God she was confident that He would. After all, God healed the pain. He dried the tears, and molded her into the woman she loves again, the one who is now stronger and wiser, the one who looks forward to her future, the one who has discovered her purpose and gained many blessings, the one who wouldn't change a thing.

She knew what she wanted and she went after it. She carried an umbrella for the rain and said a prayer for the pain and through it all she remained sane.

I thank God for rejection because without it I just wouldn't be the woman I am inside and never did I think I would say this. My experiences have been real, the tears have been real, the pain has been real, the mental trauma has been real, but when I tell you God has been the realest, He has! Dealing with people you'll be like, "who is this woman?" wondering where you lost yourself but with God you will be like "who is this woman?!" amazed at how far He has brought you.

*She never let her circumstances
cripple her because she
understood the importance of
finding the bright side of things.
Like a caterpillar enclosed within
a cocoon, she prepared to come
out of it all beautiful as ever and
ready to take flight.*

Chapter 5

The Woman Who is Ashamed

It can be very difficult to pick your head up when you're ashamed to see anyone much less talk about yourself or your life. Sometimes things happen in life that literally make us want to withdraw from the communication that we actually need with others. At the time we just want to save ourselves from further humiliation, as if being disappointed in yourself isn't enough, the thought of it all being highlighted by others can just be too much to deal with. I am here to assure you that you are not alone. I've been there.

I was the girl who had a plan. I just knew I would have certain things and things would be certain ways by the time I was a certain age. Needless to say, things definitely didn't go that way. In fact a lot of it is completely different than I could have ever imagined. After high school I knew that wasn't the end of my scholastic endeavors. I initially started out as a nursing major at a community college and completed a little of nursing school before finding out I was pregnant. Not too long after I had my son Aedan, I got back in school but chose to attend a university, The University of Alabama at Birmingham to be exact.

At this time my son was 9 months old and I had quite a bit of school left in order to graduate, especially since I went from a community college to a university. So I jumped in head first and did the best I could. As it became time to apply for nursing school I was ready and so excited to finally be back where I had left off. Well, let's just say, after two letters of non acceptance I was beginning to really get discouraged. I started feeling like I was too old to even still be in school and still not have a degree much less still waiting to get accepted into a program. At that time I was feeling down and wondering if I was even on the right path. There I was in my mid-twenties with a child and still no stable career to support myself. That wasn't at all how I saw my life going.

During that time my prayers changed some. I began telling God that I knew He knew my true passion was to help people and how I always thought the way I would do it would be through nursing. I poured my heart out to Him and asked Him to show me a different route if there was one. I really felt like I didn't have the time to just keep applying if there was something else out there for me. Maybe the fact that I wasn't getting accepted was a sign that I needed to think outside of the box I had for myself. Not too long after this I began researching different programs at The University of Alabama at Birmingham and talking with friends and other students to become more aware of it all. Well, I was introduced to The School of Health Education with a concentration in Human Services. After reading the different career fields I could enter I began praying about it again. It really was going to be a big step for me to change my major after all of the years I spent working towards getting my degree in nursing.

I ended up making the big decision to change my major and not once did I regret it. As time went by people would ask me things like "are you still in school?" "Girl, you haven't graduated yet?" I had people make comments like "you're a professional student" and joke about how many degrees I should have by now and I never really talked about how much that bothered me to anyone. I felt like I was failing myself and my son by not having it together yet by starting on something new but I continued to press on.

There were many days that I went through a lot to make it to class and stayed up long periods of time without sleep to make sure I got my work done and took the best care of my little one. Although I had a really good support system, my responsibilities being a mother in a single parent household plus all else were big so a lot of days it would be very tough. Although I was doing something to better our life I still felt ashamed that I was not established. Needless to say the next big turn in my life would really make me want to hide my head even further. As I approached graduation I began to have problems with financial aid. Since I had spent a few semesters towards nursing the amount of aid I could receive was beginning to run out.

So there I was, a few classes from graduation, staring the fact that I may not graduate after all in the face. As that spring semester came to a close I truly had no idea what I would do. I prayed and believed that God would make a way and knew that He hadn't brought me that far to leave me. Well, He did make a way and I was able to complete a few courses that summer. I was so thrilled but it all came crashing down when I was forced to face the fact that I truly wouldn't be able to finish my final 3 courses and graduate at the time I was so very looking forward to. When I tell you that was one hard blow, please believe me. Although this situation was out of my control, I felt defeated and so ashamed. Now everyone was asking about the graduation I had talked about so much and how school was going and I wasn't even enrolled.

This added to the fact that I was in my mid-twenties, had a small child, and wasn't married. That sequence was very far from the kind of life I truly wanted for myself. At that point, daily I was filled with shame and questioned where I went wrong and how I got to where I was. Honestly, it all really got to be so much. I wasn't happy with where I was and I definitely wanted things to be so much different. I didn't like to talk about the fact that my life wasn't what I wanted, or what I knew in my heart God had for me, but I just couldn't understand or grasp what I should do other than just settle for a job and do what I had to do.

Aside from that, I sometimes felt like since I was so far away from having it together that I wasn't good enough for anyone. I thought often about the type of woman, and one-day *wife,* I wanted to be and thought that I was so very far from it. I knew what kind of life, and one-day *husband,* I wanted and cringed at the thought because I felt like I would always be so unworthy of it. I felt like things would end up being everything I didn't want them to be and that I would be living a life I never wanted to live and there was nothing I could do about it. Everything felt so out of control and I was losing hope.

Do you see how much shame can cloud your thinking? Please don't be like me. Don't let shame keep you confined. No matter how far away from your goals you are, no matter how far away from your dreams you are, no matter what went wrong, and no matter how much you can't see a way, you have to learn to be okay with the truth of your situation. Once I began accepting where I was in life and knowing and believing that although it was the truth of my life at the time, it wouldn't always be that way, I began to see clearer, which opened the door for me to begin walking in my true purpose.

You might think you have it all figured out but let me tell you that things don't always go the way you had it figured and it's so important to hold your head high even during those times. Don't put yourself down and make things feel even worse by filling your mind with all things negative. Yes, you may have made some poor choices or gone a bumpier route than necessary but there is still hope and you are still living and breathing. Even though to this day I haven't finished those three courses, I'm very confident that God most certainly didn't bring me as far as He did in vain and without a purpose.

I don't know how it will all play out but I'm not ashamed anymore. Things didn't go like I wanted them to but I'm not ashamed anymore. It's part of my story. I'm co-parenting instead of raising my son the way I truly desire but I am not ashamed. I have learned so much about myself and about being a parent, about true friendship, about working together, what it truly means to be a team, maturity, the true meaning of love and what it looks and feels like, about God's grace and how very vital it is to trust His timing and plan. It took me such a very long time to even use the words "co-parenting" because those words drove the realization that things were far from what I wanted for my life. But in that realization was another hard but beneficial realization that I'm not even ready for everything I desire. That's not a reason to be ashamed but it is, and should be, a reason to prepare.

It's very easy to fall into the wrong way of thinking about things but it's important to understand that we are like clay to a potter. We are continuously being shaped and molded and God knows when we are ready. Just because we feel things should go one way doesn't mean we are prepared for them to go that way. It doesn't mean the timing is right or that it's even the right thing for us. There are so many things we don't know about situations. We just know what we want and what we feel will make us feel better about ourselves and our lives. However, I have learned that there is so much beauty in struggle. I have learned that it's not about us, it's about God and He will use all types of people and all types of situations to help us grow to be who He created us to be.

Even as I write these words to you I'm experiencing a very trying season. Since the age of 16 I have had a car. In fact I can honestly say by the time I hit my 20s I had already had 2 of my most favorite cars. I'm a very independent-minded woman. I love to go and do things for myself and I never have been one to rely on others or ask for anything unless I absolutely needed it, and even then it's hard for me. So imagine my disappointment when I fell into this time of hardship at the age of 29. I have been without a car for most of 2015 and until I decided to give myself this release in this book not many people have been aware of this at all.

It has been so very hard but by the grace of God I haven't gone without anything I need to survive. He has people strategically placed in my life who have made this time easier for me, who have helped me, who have encouraged me, and who have believed in me. It has been uncomfortable. I have felt ashamed. I have been down and had my days of wondering when things will get better. But I can honestly say I am no longer ashamed because I know that I am doing all I can and I trust that God knows what He is doing.

Much of what you read in this book was written on these days that I have been in the house due to my circumstances and with time that I'm sure I would have spent doing something else. I didn't understand it then but now I'm certain that I never would have written as much and been able to reach as many people as I have had my circumstances been any different. I really feel like it was God's way of sitting me down to do something that He wanted me to do. I had a choice to let the enemy win over my mind, distract me, and make this time the absolute worst, most depressing time, or I could listen to that still small voice, hold on to His promises, and just walk in my purpose to the best of my ability. Sometimes there is a blessing in the midst of the storm but it takes discernment and humbleness to notice it.

So instead of drowning in shame and constantly worrying about my circumstances, although I am reminded of them daily, I recognized this as an opportunity to tell you to hold on. I know I'm not the only one going through it but listen, you don't have to *look* like what you go through or what you've been through. Don't be ashamed when you know you're doing everything to just keep your head up. Don't be ashamed when you've learned the lesson and you're doing all you can to become better than before. Don't be ashamed when the people around you seem to be doing so much better than you are. Use that as encouragement that if God did it for them, He will do it for you. If you don't, your mind will become filled with worry about what others think of you or how they feel about you. You *cannot* worry about those types of things. They are not you and never will be you. This is your life, your journey. Just make sure you are building yourself up, not tearing yourself down because as you experience different things there will be enough people attempting to tear you down. You don't need to join them. You need to understand that the hardships in life can mold you into someone who is complete and beautiful if you allow them to do so. If you refuse to hide your failures and choose to be confident in yourself no matter what you're going through, that in itself could be the blessing someone else needed to see.

I have gone through some of my roughest times since I have had this platform to share my voice and little do my readers on social media outlets like Instagram and Twitter know, sometimes as I write I'm encouraging myself, I'm talking to myself. I just thank God that I can do that and reach someone else in the process. So no, I'm no longer ashamed. Although there are days I still battle with things, I am so much more confident because I finally understand that I'm not at my destination. I'm just on the way to my destination and the scenery is uncomfortable because I'm not meant to stay here.

I encourage you to start working on ridding yourself of the shame. If you have people who are willing to help you then let them. If you have to do things you don't truly want to do then pray your way through. If you have people questioning your choices or the things going on in your life, understand that you don't have to tell them every bit of your business but also don't be so full of shame that you cover over your own worth. Just because you aren't where you want to be doesn't mean you're not worthy of it.

Use the spaces below to write down some things that you are ashamed about.

1._____

_____

_____

_____.

2._____

_____

_____

_____.

3._____

_____

_____

_____.

4._____

_____

_____

_____.

Now, I want you to begin taking the necessary steps to do your part to make the best decisions possible and pray and leave the rest with God. You can't keep beating yourself up. Make peace with those things and look ahead with confidence. You are more than a conqueror and no matter what you have written you will not be defeated.

I'm no longer ashamed. Every single setback, every single pain, every single disappointment, every single misfortune has molded me. I'm no longer ashamed of what I'm not and what I haven't accomplished. I'm proud that I didn't throw the towel in any of those days I contemplated doing so because I'm finally starting to see what it means to be broken down and built up, to not understand but to trust, and no matter what that looks like right now it definitely feels good.

Doing what's best doesn't always feel like what's best while you're doing it but you have to look at the bigger picture, the biggest picture. You have to understand that feeling uncomfortable is a good thing; it helps you move forward because the last thing you want to do is stay right where you are knowing that you were created for so much more.

You may not see it right now because you're looking around and nothing looks quite familiar but that doesn't mean that you're not headed in the right direction. Sometimes a different route to destiny is just what you needed to be equipped for everything you're destined to do, to be everything you're destined to be.

Chapter 6

The Lonely Woman

Isn't it interesting how there are billions of people in this world yet we can sometimes feel so lonely. There are various different reasons why you may feel lonely right now and, as crazy as this may sound, you are indeed in a much better place than you feel. It's uncomfortable, I know. You may feel like you don't even ask for much. All you want is family who loves, supports, and accepts you for who you are. You just want friends who are loyal and believe in you. You just want someone who loves as hard as you do and wants something real.

First let me say that none of those desires are wrong at all. We were created to have relationships with people. God set the first example by placing Adam and Eve on the earth and telling them to multiply and fill the earth so don't beat yourself up or let others make you feel like you're wrong for wanting a real family, real friends, and real love. It's all natural. But I have found that those moments when we feel isolated and uncomfortable are the times when we can learn so much about ourselves. In fact, I'm sure the difficult times in my life that I've experienced were necessary for me to get to the place of understanding that I am at now. I'm certain God had me go through those periods of isolation for a reason.

You have to understand that before you can be of any benefit to others you must first begin taking care of yourself. The fact of the matter is that you can't change people. You can't make your family accept you, but you can, and must, accept yourself. You can't make friends be loyal to you or believe in you but you must be true to yourself and believe in who you are. You can't make a man have real love for you and you surely can't make him desire marriage or a family just because that's what you want, but you can love yourself and never give up hope that one day, in God's perfect timing, you will have those desires of your heart. You are a daughter of the King of the Universe and He will provide more and better for you than you could ever provide for yourself, if you will trust Him to take care of you.

So where does that leave you? It leaves you with things you need to do for yourself so that as your life begins to take the shape of your desires you're able to give others exactly what they, and accept what you, deserve, but in a healthier way, not in a dependent way. Your happiness should never be solely dependent on anyone because the reality is that just as you can have people and things they can also be lost. You have to learn how to be whole by yourself in order to open up the door to some of the best relationships you've ever experienced. So it's time to be honest. How do you feel? Are you down because you're in a season of isolation? Does it feel unfair? Are you confused? Write it down. Use the following lines to express exactly how you feel right now, your desires and discomforts, what feels unfair, and what you are afraid of.

1._____

_____

_____

_____.

2._____

_____

_____

_____.

3._____

_____

_____

_____.

4._____

_____

_____

_____.

Now, understand that your truth is in what you wrote down. As you commit to moving forward you have to accept that this time in your life may continue to be very uncomfortable. But instead of dwelling on how it feels and who and what you don't have, focus on building yourself up. Focus on being a better person and loving yourself by yourself because the truth is that being alone doesn't have to mean feeling lonely. Keep in mind that some of what I'm saying is easier said than done but remember that that is coming from someone who has made it strides farther than she once even thought was possible. Just remember, as I will probably say again and again, *trust your journey.*

As weird as this may sound, so what you don't have any real friends right now? Go out and do some things that you love. Start a new hobby. Position yourself to meet new people. Maybe your family has decided they don't want to accept the path you've chosen for your life. Do you agree and understand that you're doing what's best for you? If so, you must begin making peace with their decision whether you agree or not by starting with simply respecting their choice. Leave the things that are too big for you with God and trust that He will sort things out for you. You don't have to have a man to go on a date. Take yourself to dinner and a movie. All of these things may sound very strange because you're still thinking that in order for these things to be fun you need someone else. Once you understand that you can have a great time by yourself you will look forward to being able to do this for yourself no matter how many people you could be doing those things with.

You have to adopt the perspective that things won't always look the way they look right now, they won't always feel the way they do right now. Grow through what you go through versus getting stuck in your negative feelings and prolonging the process. You are worthy of healthy relationships with others and you are most definitely worthy of real love. Commit to building strength and making the best of this season of your life as preparation for the greater things that are to come. As you begin to grow, look back at the things you wrote on the lines in this section and smile at how you're feeling. Be proud of how far you have come.

As you move forward always remember that God is there for you and so very willing to restore your peace, mend your broken heart, and fill the void that you live with daily. You are never truly alone even when you feel alone; even as you begin to start putting the things you've read to action. He is there to be the ultimate source of understanding and comfort. I know that He is the reason I'm able to tell you these things because when I felt alone He stepped in and showed me what I needed to do. Although there are still tough days, taking on a new perspective and trusting God is the way to go so be encouraged.

You don't need a romantic relationship to be happy. Skip to the rhythm of your own beat and be grateful for the gift of life.

Many days she felt she was alone but she never was. God was always watching over her. Even when she had fallen so low and no one was around to even notice, He kept her.

Enjoy that quiet time and look forward to tomorrow, it will be a blessing. Every day that you've been working on yourself has been beautiful, even when it felt rough. You are doing just fine. Your journey is designed to shape and mold you to be equipped to walk in purpose and every day you shine just a little brighter and become a little more put together. It's so beautiful that you've chosen to be better on purpose.

Within those quiet moments, those moments that you so passionately wish were filled with voices and laughter from loved ones, there is purpose. There is opportunity. There is the opportunity for you to recognize that maybe you are right where you need to be to learn exactly what you need to learn, to grow. So just go with the flow.

Chapter 7

The Woman Who Can't Forgive

A lot of people travel their journey through life feeling like forgiveness is for the other person. It's almost like they don't forgive because they feel like if they do forgive it gives the person who did them wrong something that they don't deserve. But the truth is that forgiveness is for yourself. It's just so hard to grasp that truth at times because we can become focused on the wrong things. However, the sooner you focus on choosing better over allowing bitterness to grow, your life will take a turn for the better.

You have to forgive in order to move forward, so ultimately you hold the power within your grasp. You can be one of the best people to walk this earth and someone will still treat you wrongly. Bad things do in fact happen to good people and they don't always get an apology. Maybe you never got that apology and the wounds are still open. If that's the case, it's time to start healing and understand that as crazy as it may sound you can forgive someone without them ever asking you to forgive them and without them ever saying "I'm sorry." It starts within; it starts with understanding that you didn't deserve the ill treatment and that even though you were wronged your life does go on.

The best way to go on is in peace and that's where the forgiveness comes in. Forgiveness equals peace. I don't know your story. Maybe you're having trouble forgiving your father who left you or your mother who never loved you the way you deserved. Maybe your ex cheated or maybe someone led you on. Maybe someone you placed so much trust in let you down. Whatever you may be going through, know that better days are truly ahead and you deserve every minute of it so you must commit to healing now. If you're anything like me, you, without even thinking, see the good in people. While seeing the good you have to also understand that we all make poor choices and do things that we shouldn't do. Thankfully, by the grace of God we are forgiven when we ask for forgiveness and truly repent.

We have to learn to truly cherish the grace and mercy bestowed upon us in order to genuinely be able to forgive others. Once we do that we begin to look at things from a different perspective. Consider this, they hurt you, maybe they left you, maybe they said the worst things possible to you and now they have gone on with their life leaving you behind in pain. Now you are left to pick up the pieces. Cherish yourself enough to say, "okay, it happened, but I must move forward." Remember that forgiveness doesn't mean you have to open your life up to them again and it doesn't mean that you're saying it was okay for them to do what they did. You can make peace with wrongs done to you and move on without them yet still have forgiven the individual who caused you harm. Forgiveness means no longer holding on to the wrong and choosing to no longer hold it against them, to no longer let the wrong have a hold on you. Forgiveness ushers in peace.

When you don't forgive you begin to transfer blame to yourself, so before you know it you start saying things like "it's my fault" and "I'm so stupid." It's a way of trying to make sense of things but the truth is that not everything will make sense and you are going to have to learn to accept that. So much of this journey to forgiveness has to do with trusting the process, even though it is very uncomfortable, and allowing yourself to grow from your experiences instead of remaining complacent with them. One of the most important things you need to do is face what *really* hurt you most. Understanding your own feelings will help you get closer to the point of genuine forgiveness.

Use the lines below to come face to face with what you are truly feeling inside. Write down who hurt you, what they did, and the *real* reasons it hurt you so badly.

1._____

_____

_____

_____

_____.

2._____

_____

_____

_____

_____.

3._____

_____

_____

_____

_____.

    Now that you have written it down say a prayer and commit to letting it go. Commit to understanding that there is nothing you can do at this point to change what happened but that you can change how you let it affect you. Commit to not allowing bitterness to grow, commit to loving yourself enough to move forward, and concentrate on treating others how you would like to be treated. I am a firm believer that when you put out good, good comes back to you. Maybe not right away but it *will* come back to you.

    Remember that you can't control people's actions but you can control your reaction to their actions. The very best thing you can do is move forward and be a living witness that although you have been wronged you're stronger than ever and still working towards becoming better each day despite anything and everything designed to tear you down. Once you begin learning how to handle situations better you will find you're much less stressed when other things arise, which allows you to learn so much more about yourself through the situation. All of this combined will make forgiving others in the future so much easier. You will have grasped the fact that you need to do it for yourself because peace will always be much better than pain and pain can't be healed without forgiveness.

There will be times when all you want to do is curl into a ball and cry because you're constantly reminded of their lies; you're constantly reminded of how bad it hurts but you have to learn to put yourself first. That's what it means to forgive and once you do that you will begin to live, again.

She thought it was just for them but it was for her. It was so that she could breathe again. And she could breathe not just any kind of air, not air polluted with bitterness and pain, but pure and fresh air. It was because she deserved to live her days freely; not bound to her past. Yes, she found freedom in forgiveness.

Chapter 8

The Woman Who Makes Excuses

Do you often find yourself saying "but" when it comes to making decisions or when things aren't going your way? Whatever the case may be, making excuses is one of the number one ways to find yourself exactly where you are right now in the years to come. I get it; sometimes it's so hard to find the determination to do what you need to do. Sometimes you feel defeated because you feel like you have given it all you have but see little or no results at all so you lose the willpower to try again and the faith to keep praying.

That's real life. It happens and the one thing about excuses is that when we begin to make them we lose sight of whether they are just excuses or the truth. Oftentimes it becomes our truth and that's a dangerous thing. For every situation there is a solution. Even if the problem is too big for us to solve on our own we can always go to God in prayer. Even in doing that we must understand accountability. Sometimes we are the reason for our own problems. Yes, it takes being super transparent with yourself to accept that you are the reason why you are in certain situations. You can't blame other people forever, because guess what? Those very same people will have gone on with their life while you are still stuck in what happened. At some point you need to be able to say "I messed up" and not just stop right there but work hard to do what you can to make things better.

You can't blame that man who broke your heart for the rest of your life and use that as an excuse to give up on love or not give any other man a chance. Who is the one hurting the most when you do that? It's you. You are blocking the possibility of something beautiful transpiring in your life by mistaking your excuses for truth. No, it's not easy to open up and give someone else a chance but you have to first know in your heart and mind that you deserve to be loved and appreciated and that not all men are the exact same. They don't all do what "he" did. They won't all do what "he" did.

You can't get comfortable with putting off what you need to do today for tomorrow because before you know it so much time will have gone by and absolutely no progress will have been made. You can't build a greater life on the idea that another day will be better than the one you are living right now. You build with the idea that every single day is another opportunity to do something else that's in the direction of your dreams. Food doesn't cook itself, homes don't build themselves, organizations aren't run on their own, clothes don't make themselves, books don't write themselves, relationships don't mend themselves, degrees aren't received without hard work, and that business won't build itself. Your purpose can't be carried out if you don't move.

Never give another person or a situation so much power over you that you let it hold you back. *Do*

not do that! Yes, it is easier said than done but it is possible to rise above your circumstances and the things that have happened to you. If you hold on to whatever it is that has you stuck right where you are then it will always control your life. Maybe you didn't have your father in your life and you have insecurities and trust issues. That's a very big deal and will fill your life with toxic fumes that will suffocate you from seeing your worth as long as you hold on to it.

The fact of the matter is you can't go back and change how things were, or how things are for that matter. By the grace of God you are where you are right now and you made it to this day without him. There could be so many different reasons why he left but none of them make it okay for you to disrespect yourself for attention or settle for less because you don't feel you deserve more. Your lack doesn't grant you permission to make things even more unfortunate. That's not an excuse to become complacent. You have to now take responsibility for your life starting with making peace with your truth. God knows exactly what you were, or are, lacking and He will fill that void for you. He will help you heal those insecurities but you have to first stop with the excuses and commit to healing from your past.

Maybe you are like me and you grew up in a very loving, two parent household but now you have a child of your own and you're single, raising your child in a one parent household. You know the saying is true that we want better for our children than we had ourselves so there are days where you feel awful because you feel like you can't even provide them with what you had. You feel so less than; you truly feel like the tail and you are so far from the head. I'll be the very first to say that it's heartbreaking but you have to take responsibility for your part in things and again, *make peace with your truth.*

You can't let it be an excuse to not be the very best mother you can be and, if your child's father is active in your child's life, then thank God for that and don't let the fact that you two aren't together anymore be an excuse for you to keep up drama and make it hard for him to be the father that your child needs. You can't let your past pain be an excuse to disrupt the peace you deserve. You can't let your circumstances be an excuse to put yourself down. Believe it or not your children pick up on your daily vibes. If you don't get it together they will soon start taking on those depressing negative vibes. Children are so resilient and so are you. Maybe the family you desired is broken and maybe this was never the way you wanted things to be but at this very moment, this is your life. You just have to know that *This Isn't It!*

Don't get so wrapped up in how you feel and how things are that you fail to pray for better. Listen, it starts with you. You have to desire to first be a better woman and mother before placing your concentration on being someone's future wife. Being a mother before marriage isn't an excuse to *continue* to skip steps. Sometimes we have to go back to who we were before our lives were forever changed and work on *her,* that *woman within.*

Even before you became a mother you were a woman and that woman still needs to grow, be humbled, shaped, and molded into the best she can be. Do that! Work on that all while being the very best mother you can be. Being right where you are isn't an excuse to stay there no matter how old you are or how old your child is. *This Isn't It!* Just like you want better, God wants better for you, and just because you did it out of order isn't an excuse for you to continue that trend. God can bless you with a wonderful man to be a beautiful example for your child to see how He created the family circle and to see how you deserve to be loved. But in the meantime, drop any of the excuses you've been using to remain in the negative place you may be in mentally. Love yourself and your child enough to make good and wise choices going forward.

You know, sometimes we just feel like we were dealt a bad hand and that everyone else has an advantage over us. I'm not here to say whether or not that's true but I am here to say that even if it feels like all odds are against you it's not an excuse for you to settle. Your mind is so much more powerful than you think. Start saying things like "I didn't have anyone to help me get started but I'm going to start and I'm going to give this the best I can." That is an example of changing your perspective because you won't get anywhere thinking that just because something is going to be harder for you than you feel it is for someone else you can't do it. To be honest, the fact that you may have to put forth so much more effort will make you appreciate it all so much more.

Your self-reflection has been saved for the end this time. Use the spaces provided to write down your top four excuses.

1._____

_____

_____

_____.

2._____

_____

_____

_____.

3._____

_____

_____

_____.

4._____

_____

_____

_____.

It doesn't feel like it when you are going through it but I have observed some of the most important people to me go through some of the toughest times that you could imagine and I found so much beauty in their struggle. Not that they had to struggle, but that their resilience and faith in God carried them through. It's no different for you. You have to want better for your life. Your desire has to overpower your feelings of defeat. Your faith has to overpower your fear and you can't let your excuses overpower your effort.

She made excuses and they were
useless.

They kept her hidden behind bars,
restricted from her own potential.

All she seemed to focus on were
the things she'd been through.

If she could just get out of her own
way she could see that God
already made sure everything was
okay.

Excuses are like a pill filled with poison, every time you accept one it's like you're swallowing something that will slowly put an end to your life. The life you were meant to live.

Some excuses are justifiable but some just scream laziness and defeat. Some just hold you back from being everything you were created to be.

Chapter 9

The Woman Who Is Waiting

As women we are so resilient. It amazes me how hard we love and how tight we hold on to the people and things that have our hearts. Sometimes you find yourself holding on, unsure if you should let go or clench tighter and sometimes that hurts. None of us are immune to these types of situations. All you have to have is a big heart, which is something I feel so many of us have, and as bad as it may seem, and much as that may seem to be a curse, it's really a blessing.

Don't beat yourself up because you're having a hard time moving on. And don't be hard on yourself if you're just truly unsure if you should wait or let go. Take time to understand why you want to hold on and face the reasons why you should let go. You have to understand that you cannot change a man. Nothing you do will ever be good enough for a man who isn't ready. You can treat him like the King he may not even realize he is yet and still be left feeling alone. It doesn't matter how much of yourself you've given or how hard you have fought to make it work. When it's all said and done it takes two people who want the same things. Some people train themselves to be okay settling in a place in which they know they don't truly want to be. You can't continue on pretending like you don't see that there is no progression. You can't keep feeling alone knowing that they really don't love you the way they would need to in order for it to work. You want to hold on because they are what you want, but what about what you need? Doesn't that actually matter most?

This is a situation where the bad can truly outweigh the good but because we are human and have desires we cling to whatever good is present and go blind to the bad. This is why I encourage you to truly be real with yourself about *everything*. One of the keys to a good life is honesty, yet so often we are more honest with others than we are with ourselves. I just have to be real with you. I have learned that at times the only one we should wait on is God and that doesn't mean you don't love that man in every way. It doesn't mean you don't love him in the deepest ways. That just means that you accept that the situation is too big for you. You understand that you are at your most vulnerable state and ultimately just want what's best for yourself and you can be totally honest and say "whatever that is". You don't have to figure it all out on your own. Your faith needs to be in overdrive. You have to trust this journey and know that you deserve a clearer mind.

Communication is everything, so talk to that man and find out what he really wants, how he really feels, and what he really wants to do, while making it clear that you love him but don't want to waste your time or his living like all is well while you both know that it isn't. You also have to have a very good mind of your own and make sure that their actions match their words. You don't wait around for things to change or get better when all signs show no improvement and no efforts towards a change. The truth is that we go hard for the people and the things that we want. Even if that truth speaks to you and says "they don't really care", you have to accept it. The facts speak for themselves and they will be the same tomorrow and the day after that.

That's not to say that they don't care at all but they don't care *enough* in the way needed to do what it takes to keep you in their life, and not only keep you, but take care of you in all of the ways two people should care for each other. You know right now that you've probably traveled to the moon and back for them and probably selflessly. You deserve someone who loves you like that, someone who will do the same. Men are supposed to find a good thing. The truth is sometimes they find that good thing and instead of holding on tight they handle it very carelessly.

Think about it like a child with a $100 bill. That child doesn't have a real understanding of the value of that money so instead of making smart choices with it they waste it on things that won't even last. A man who doesn't understand the value of a good woman will not make the best decisions when it comes to her. He hasn't grown and matured enough to know what he has. So a lot of times it's him, not you. But as women we beat ourselves up wondering "what's wrong with me?" "Why am I not good enough?" not understanding that he just doesn't understand how good you are. Unfortunately, you can't do anything to speed up that process.

Sometimes a man sees every bit of the woman you are and knows that he isn't where he needs to be to embrace you fully. Men experience fear just like we do. Sometimes they feel that they're not enough and that they can't give you what you need or be the type of man they feel you deserve. Even when you feel that they are more than enough and that they deserve every bit of who you are, that doesn't change a thing. Love doesn't work that way. No matter how they feel, they have to be *willing* to open up and embrace you for who you are, right where you are, *and right where they are,* and you can't wait forever to see if that will happen. You can't wait forever for them to see their own worth and the potential of your relationship.

A man has to know who he is in order to know who you are. He needs to be happy with himself in order to be happy with you. There is nothing wrong with being there for a man and giving your relationship your all, but you have to know when it's time to walk away and believe it or not, walking away doesn't have to be the end of your story. Now, I may go against everything you've ever been told when I say this, but what a lot of us do is write "the end" after walking away when really we should insert "God's will" as we move forward. That means, "God, I don't understand this, I don't know what will happen, I don't really even understand what has happened, but I know that you know best and this is now all yours." Let Him be the author and finisher. It's up to us to be humble and obedient.

Sometimes you just have to take your hands out of it and shift your attention to working on yourself and your life and trust God to bless you with who He has for you at the perfect time. Let Him do His work in you and trust that He will do His work in whomever your companion will be. We are all on a journey and understanding our worth is one of the biggest things we will do. We sometimes say that we deserve the best but we don't all do what it takes to be ready for, and to receive, the best. Don't hold on tightly when the grip is hurting you deeply. Move forward saying "God's will" and place your concentration on walking in your God-given purpose, because when you do that everything else will fall in place in His perfect timing. You deserve it Queen! You deserve to be happy, and you deserve to have that beautiful love that you give to others. If you can just allow God to BE God you will begin to believe that everything will be okay.

He was surely a piece to her puzzle and her favorite piece, but he just couldn't see how he fit so perfectly

To all of you who are hurting let me tell you how great God is. If one puzzle piece refuses to see that it fits so perfectly He will shape and mold another piece that will. Now, have your moment, cry if you have to, but when you pick your head up trust that God has you, your life is in His hands, and He will make sure that everything comes together just right ***no matter what.***

Not every man wants a family and not every man appreciates one. Not every man appreciates a good woman, not to mention a good woman who is also a mother. Understand that not every man is the same so just like one doesn't, another one will.

The relationship will only grow stronger when two people understand that it's no longer about just them and they love that fact. Be with someone who wants a bond that they never want to break.

We go hard for who and what matters. If they don't go hard for you then let it tell you something.

She waited because she cared.

She didn't move on because she was scared,

Scared to lose someone who meant so much,

Scared to feel like she didn't hold on long enough.

It all just hurt,

But in the end she had to put herself first.

She had to know her worth.

You can be the sweetest, most caring, most giving, most loving, most supportive woman but if he doesn't want you none of that will ever make a difference. Having a desire for you to be in his life is vital.

I won't beg a single soul to love me, appreciate me, or see me for the woman I am. I'm not perfect, or even close, but underneath my flaws and shortcomings is a woman who loves fiercely, one who desires to add, build, and grow. I will ride to the end for someone who desires and appreciates that. So no, it doesn't even sound sane to beg someone to appreciate something so real.

Chapter 10

The Self Conscious Woman

From the time most of us were born we had smiling faces hovering over us telling us how incredibly adorable we were. As we grew older, even if others were cruel at least our mother, father, someone in our family, or someone close to us told us that we were beautiful just the way we were and it helped in more ways than one. As we grow into adults though, we should be at a place where we truly love and believe in ourselves because nobody can do that for us. We get to a place where what others say doesn't matter as much as how we feel so how we feel is most important. Therefore, we have to be very careful as to the beliefs we adopt. As women we are constantly being told how we should look, what size we should be, what kind of makeup we should wear, how we should or shouldn't do our hair. It's just a constant push to fit in with the masses and while this may not always be a bad fit for us it can definitely be detrimental if you begin thinking less of yourself because you aren't how you have been programmed to feel you should look.

That's why I say the emphasis is on what you personally believe. Let's just be real, we are all made differently. We are different shapes, sizes, and skin tones. That is what makes us all unique. You are the only person living in the skin you're in so you need to learn to be comfortable there. If you don't like your hair, change it. If you want to wear makeup, wear it, if you don't, don't. If you don't like your weight, get up and do something about it. Just don't let what someone else says be your only influence to make a change. You have to be happy with yourself and as long as you are happy and healthy nothing else should matter.

Take a moment to really be honest with yourself. On the lines below I want you to write down the top things that you're self-conscious about. Don't sugar coat it; pour out your heart. Reveal those things you usually don't speak about.

1._____

_____

_____

_____.

2._____

_____

_____

_____.

3._____

_____

_____

_____.

It truly helps to get things out and then take steps forward. The only way we can progress is by facing exactly what's affecting us and determining a healthy way of dealing with it all. I want you to keep the things you have written down in mind as you read this chapter. Understand that you are not alone in your feelings. Before you can accept any advice or see any truth you have to accept that you are a human with feelings first.

Personally, I'm at a place right now where I just want to be happy with the woman I am no matter what anyone else thinks. I'm pushing the age of 30 and have picked up a few too many pounds *in my opinion* so I'm trying to take steps to get to a place where I feel most comfortable. But in the meantime it's not always the most pleasant. Some days I look in the mirror and I'm like "When did I start gaining weight there?" or "Ugh, when will I see results?" That's just the transparent truth but it doesn't make the mentality right. Doing that never helps me lose a single inch, it only makes the time I spend at the weight I'm at a little bit bumpier. I've learned that the key is just to work hard to get where you want to be and be as positive as you can along the journey. Don't spend even one second of your time comparing yourself to others or putting yourself down. One thing I have found is that excuses are the easiest at this point. Trust me, I battle with that, but I know what it takes to get any type of result and that's a change.

What you have to understand is that even that person who you think is flawless indeed has flaws. We all do. It's all in your perspective and how you *choose* to feel. Don't get complacent if there is something you don't like that you can indeed change. But for those things that can't really be changed, you must learn to embrace them because they are part of what makes you who you are. As women I feel like we have too much placed on us to look "beautiful". But what exactly is beauty? It is indeed in the eye of the beholder. You need to be the very first person to see yourself as beautiful.

Don't let what you have been through make you feel "less than". People are always going to have something to say whether you're doing good or bad. One of the most important things to understand is that we all are on a journey. Some of us have a past that is unknown by many, while others have a past that others can point at and have an opinion, but at the end of the day, it's all still the *past*. You don't live there anymore. Forgive yourself because if you have repented and asked God for forgiveness then He has already forgiven you. Who are you to not forgive yourself when The God of the Universe loves and forgives you? What are you waiting for? Let it go and embrace the woman you are right now.

Beauty reaches so far beyond what we see in the mirror, far deeper than the imperfections that we cover over. It extends so far beyond our past. We all have flaws but it's so much better to work on them as you move forward than to sit and let what you don't like about yourself consume you. Get up! Change what you can but place the *most* emphasis on your inner self. So many of us let what others think define us. You are absolutely not your past or what others see on the surface. God defines you Queen! See yourself as He sees you. Reach within and commit to healing because you deserve it, then look in the mirror with confidence because you are still standing even after all of the hell you've been through. You are the greatest and today is the day to begin building the ultimate confidence *in* yourself.

Chapter 11

The Gentlewoman

I don't know about you but there have been times in my life when I wished that I didn't have the big heart that I have, times I wished that I wasn't such a gentle being. I wished that I didn't care as deeply as I do. I wished that I could have that "I don't care" attitude that I see so many people displaying. I wished that I was heartless and the only reason I wished such things was because I was hurting so badly inside after the end of a relationship. Nothing really made sense to me.

I felt like I had given all I had. In fact now I know I did, but at the time I couldn't understand why that wasn't enough. I couldn't understand why we couldn't just work at the things we faced, overcome them together, let it all go, and move forward. The easiest thing seemed to be just not caring at all but I'm no good at that. I'm not wired that way. I value commitment. I'm loyal and when I love I love hard.

It was so very tough facing things that I didn't want to accept. I had opened my heart so wide, wider than ever before. I had never loved so unconditionally, and to me, when you truly love someone you'll fight for them and for the relationship you have together. I went through all types of feelings and emotions. There were days when I thought I felt good, only to be followed by others where I would crumble into pieces, like literally break all the way down. It was so hard, so many days.

Everything could have gone so many different ways but I am truly able to testify that being true to yourself is a real blessing despite it all.

When things don't go the way we want them to go we immediately begin to feel emotions, and definitely not the best ones. Emotions are the one thing I will say are very hard to control when you're in pain, especially for a woman who's accustomed to being peaceful and patching things up. You become very unsure what to do when you feel everything other than gentle inside and you feel like there's nothing you can do. You have to get hold of those emotions though, or at least control them, so as to not directly affect the sensitive situation in a more negative way. I had a really hard time with that in the beginning, but as time has passed, and with God's help, I have gotten better at dealing with how I am feeling within. It was nothing I could do on my own.

Instead of letting the devil in to have his way, I began to see his attacks and react in a way which required more personal growth on my behalf. You have to understand that any time you are trying to do something that involves peace and positivity, Satan works hard to interrupt that process. So he definitely wasn't happy to see me thinking clearer and doing the things that were right for me. I'm sure he wanted all out chaos but I wasn't about to be a part of giving him what he wanted. It took a lot of growing on my behalf to get to where I am today and that struggle had nothing to do with anyone other than myself. There was so much God needed to do within me while I thought I had it so together. Every single thing that I went through helped mold me into who I am today but it was far from easy battling my deep feelings and shattered dreams. It all has taught me so much about understanding what matters most, and what is important is being obedient to God.

Over the years I have learned a lot about myself. I can honestly say that I am glad that God didn't give me what I wanted when I wanted it. I even appreciate everything that I have learned and experienced. No, I am not living the life I saw for myself and things are not how I wanted them to be, but I trust this journey now. Every single thing in your life won't go the way you want it to go and some things you go through will be to teach you everything you need to be prepared for the things that are on the way. Trust this journey Queen. As hard as it may be, don't lose that gentle spirit. Don't turn into that woman you know you're not meant to be. Do what's best for yourself. Let that be the fuel you need to get over the fuel to make poor choices; let that be your desire to hold on. Let that be what inspires you to remain gentle and let God do the work in you that needs to be done.

Don't worry about what everyone else is doing. Do what *you* need to do. Everything happens for a reason and don't worry about what people will think or what they will say about your choices. You are not everyone else and if you worry about trying to do things that make sense to them you'll mess up and do things that aren't meant for you. Always be true to yourself and listen to that still small voice. Sometimes God pulls at our heart strings to do things we may not quite understand at that time, but just trust Him.

Being true to yourself just might be what launches you into some of the best days of your life because it positions you for growth right where you are and with the beautiful characteristics with which God has already blessed you. Again, sometimes what we feel is a curse, like our big hearts, is really a blessing. If you allow the devil to distract you then you will begin acting out of character, and when you do that, it makes the process so much longer. I encourage you to endure those difficult times; please *hold on*. Trust me, I have been there. I went to sleep with a wet pillow many nights and woke up wondering "why me?" I have been broken and confused but I assure you there is a beautiful lesson to be learned through all of the chaos. You aren't going through it alone, so the quicker you accept who you are and what you're going through, the more open you will be to getting help, whether it be by God directly or through someone God sends your way. May God continue to bless all of you Gentlewomen.

Have you ever experienced a love so deep and heartbreak so painful that you tried to pray the love away but no matter how hard you prayed it felt like that love was there to stay?...And all you knew was that it hurt so bad.

Sometimes we lose the ones we
never wanted to lose,
The ones we fought to keep
And that pain cuts so deep.
The pain makes you lose sleep,
You're left tasting defeat.
Your heart left feeling like some
things are meant,
Your mind knowing they'll never
be.

Everything won't always make sense. As bad as you want it to, the truth is you don't need it to make sense right now. What you need is peace and that's something you receive when you just accept that God knows better than you do and let it all rest within His hands.

Chapter 12

This Isn't It

When you're going through the toughest times of your life you're being shaped and molded. You're gaining precious strength. You're growing while feeling so small and you'll become whole again after being so broken. Listen, you can't pray away a love that was genuine and came from a good place. It doesn't work like that. If anything, just be proud of yourself for giving it all you had, for being able to love someone so unconditionally. Some have no idea what that kind of love even means. Even through the pain you're experiencing right now you actually know what it means to love, and some people die without ever experiencing such a thing. You just have to heal. It may be that you'll always love that person, but you'll just move past the pain that you feel from having to do life without them. Right now all you know is that it hurts so bad, but know that you can get through anything with God's help. It's true. If He did it for me, He can do it for you.

Things don't end here. Even when you feel like you have reached your end, the fact of the matter is that you haven't. That is the time to drop to your knees and ask for help. It doesn't matter what you're going through, how long you've been going through it, or how bad it hurts. Nothing at all is too big for God. I think back on some of the toughest times of my life and I'm so thankful that I didn't give up when I felt like it; and there were plenty of times when I wanted to. Now it all makes so much more sense to me. My tough times prepared me to be able to let someone else know that they can make it too. There have been plenty of days where I felt like things would never get better. I felt like I would never stop feeling so crushed. I didn't think I would ever get to do the things that made my heart the happiest, like what I'm doing right now. Yet here I am. It happened and it all made me so much stronger.

There is no way I can count how many times I've heard God telling me "This Isn't It" and how many times I have told myself "This Isn't It". Life itself is something to be thankful for but when you have a great purpose inside, you will never feel comfortable settling where you know you don't belong. I am thankful for every single thing I have but I just know that this isn't it for me. There is more to life, more for me to experience, a better life to live, and the very same goes for you. Whatever the situation is you have to look past it and know that things will absolutely not always be as they are right now. Things happen and it really is a choice to give up or rise up.

As I began writing this book I was so very happy inside. Finally I was doing something that I once only mentioned I wanted to do one day. I wrote and wrote and wrote some more all the way up until I lost my flash drive that had all that I had written on it and I hadn't saved the files anywhere else. I searched and searched and searched some more for it, only to be devastated by not finding it. It crushed my spirit. All of my hard work was missing and now I was facing starting over or giving up. I cried and prayed and told myself that I would not let myself down. I would not give up and I would not let that setback cause me to change the time period I wanted to bring this book to you. I remember taking a deep breath and saying that if I did it once I could do it again.

After the tears and tearing my home and purses apart looking for my flash drive, I can honestly say that I feel it all happened for a reason, a good one. As I was writing to you all on Instagram, and even writing parts of this book, I was going through it myself, but I promised myself that I wouldn't let that stop me from writing, I wouldn't let it cause me to put my passion on hold or push my goal back. You see, things don't always go the way we want them to, in fact, sometimes they painfully go a different way, but the only way that becomes the end is if you let it. I am not here to tell you that it's easy. I will say that time and time again because clearly it isn't, by any means, but it is possible. You have to let everything you experience teach you something and it's essential that you discipline yourself accordingly. You have to understand and accept the way things go in life sometimes, and although you may not like it or agree with it, it's life. Your job is to be determined not to let anything stand in the way of you and your purpose for being on this earth, and if you don't know what that is yet it's time for you to get up and begin to figure it out.

We get this one precious life but unfortunately sometimes we spend it learning lessons we should've learned so long ago, and making mistakes that turn into intentional choices. Don't fall into the trap of feeling like just because nobody around you has risen above the obstacles in their life that you can't. Don't feel like just because you lost something good that something far better isn't headed your way. Don't think that because one person didn't see your worth nobody will. Listen, this isn't *it* for you. That bad news isn't *it*, your unfortunate circumstances isn't *it*, that illness you are battling isn't *it*. You still have breath in your body which means purpose is still running through your veins. Get excited about life again because the time you spend with your head held completely down is time you spend missing what's already in front of you and you make it impossible to see any hope for a brighter future.

It's time to revive that woman within, she's there. Sometimes we allow pain, anger, frustration, and even bitterness, just to name a few, to cause us to become someone we are totally not. We lose ourselves and begin to tuck away the beautiful things that make us amazing women. We begin stripping ourselves bit by bit and piece by piece until we feel like nothing is left within us. Don't let that happen any longer because the one hurting the most is you and you don't deserve to let that pain win another day. You are greater than depression and anxiety. It can all have a very powerful hold over you but that hold doesn't have to last forever. The sooner you begin to accept yourself for who you are and where you are the sooner you can open the door to change. You can't change things if you won't open your eyes to even see that there's a problem. Don't make excuses for your bad choices and most definitely don't make excuses for not doing something about it all.

Things happen as life happens every second. We don't have control over every single thing that happens, but we do have control over how we react to it. It's time to start reacting like a woman with faith. That means, even if you don't see your way you trust your guide. You do every single thing you can to make things better, and for all else you have to place it in God's hands and move on to doing the next great thing. Just because something goes wrong doesn't mean you can't shift your attention over to something else and begin doing the best you can with it. I know it feels like when it rains it pours but all of that rain only prepares your life for growth. You don't see it at the time, but just keep pushing. You will begin to see growth within yourself and in different areas of your life.

Without rain there would be a drought and in a drought all living things begin to perish. We need the rain to enjoy the beautiful days. You need to learn certain lessons and be humbled in certain ways in order to start reaching your true potential. So the next time you are faced with something difficult, I want you to tell yourself that this isn't *it* for you and make it a point to act in accordance with your affirmation. When you know that whatever you're facing isn't *it* for you, then you make decisions that reflect that. Don't let the beautiful Queen within you lay lifeless as you go through life carelessly broken with barely any trace of the beautiful woman God created you to be in sight.

Remember where true beauty is; it is within. Commit to being happier, healthier, and purposeful. All of that requires you to know your worth. That same worth that you may have lost sight of along your journey is still there. Find it. Never lose it. Never settle and never give up.